10X1,000,000

Your Path to Success and Transformation

Aladdin X

Copyright © 2024 Aladdin X

All rights reserved.

This book cannot be reproduced or transmitted in any form or by any means, electronic or mechanical, including photocopying, recording, or by any information 1 storage and retrieval system, without written permission from the 2 author.

ISBN: 9798304712507

Published by: Independently published

Author: Aladdin X

First Edition

© 2024 Aladdin X

Table of Contents

10X1,000,000: Your Path to Success and Transformation 4

10X1,000,000 5

X1: Acknowledgment 6

X2: The Leaks 10

X3: Flow 14

X4: Leadership 18

X5: Pretending 23

X6: Temporal Preference 27

X7: Multiplication 32

X8: Selection 36

X9: The Center of the Circle 41

X10: The Golden Standard 45

10X1,000,000: Implementation 51

10X1,000,000: Your Path to Success and Transformation

Are you ready to transform your reality?

Within each of us lies boundless ambition, often stifled by the habits and constraints of daily life. In this book, you will uncover how to take control of your life, becoming the author of your unique journey to success.

What You Will Discover in This Book:

1. The Beginning: Upgrade Your Internal System

    Learn how to break free from old habits and adopt a mindset for success.

2. Seal Financial Leaks

    Identify habits that drain your financial resources and learn how to redirect them toward meaningful goals.

3. Make Your Life a River of Flow

    Discover how to create multiple streams of income for a more stable and prosperous life.

4. Lead Your Money: Control Before Earning

    Master the art of managing your finances instead of letting them control you.

5. Balancing Choices

    Explore the art of selecting opportunities, relationships, and decisions that align with your goals.

6. The Strategy of Multiplication

    Learn how to grow your efforts and finances intelligently to achieve sustainable wealth.

This book is more than words on a page; it is an invitation to take bold steps toward a better future. Success does not wait—it begins with your decision now.

10X1,000,000

Within the heart of every individual lies an unbounded ambition, yet it is often suffocated under the weight of daily habits and the constraints we impose upon ourselves. We speak of success, we seek it, but do we possess the courage to confront it? The harsh truth is: success does not run away from you; it is you who flee from it when you hesitate to make bold decisions.

There comes a pivotal moment in every person's life—a moment when they decide to stop being a mere spectator of their own life and instead become the true author of their future story. That moment does not come from luck or coincidence but from courageous awareness, a decision born from within: *"I will no longer be a prisoner of my circumstances; I will become their master."*

Life is not a game of chance or a basket of ready-made resources handed to you. It is a game of strategies, a game you win when you learn how to seal the gaps that drain your energy, how to amplify your value by directing your resources wisely, and how to create new opportunities instead of waiting for them to appear.

For the greatest truth of all says: *"The world owes you nothing, but it will give you everything if you have the courage to claim it."*

And that is what you are about to discover: how to become the maestro of your own life, the conductor of your flows, and the creator of your unique path to success.

X1: Acknowledgment

Upgrade Your Internal System: Change Begins with the Mind

Imagine using an outdated phone—one that drains your time and energy. You find yourself wishing for a newer device, one that works faster and offers a smoother, more efficient experience. Why do we buy new phones? Not just because they look better, but because they provide better features and make our lives easier.

Now, ask yourself this: Do your thoughts need an upgrade as well? Are you still navigating life with an old mental operating system that no longer serves your goals? If your answer is "yes," welcome to the first step toward transformation.

Facing the Truth

Before anything else, you must admit: your current situation is the direct result of your past thoughts, behaviors, and decisions. Every small choice you made, every habit you adopted, every moment of denial or procrastination contributed to shaping this reality. Acknowledging this isn't a sign of weakness or defeat—it is the bravest act you can take.

If you are entirely satisfied with your financial state, you wouldn't be holding this book in your hands or searching for answers. That alone proves there is a gap between where you are and where you want to be. Recognizing that gap means you understand there's room for improvement. If you can't admit that, close this book now—change is not for those who deny responsibility.

Why Acknowledge?

Acknowledgment is the key to unlocking the door to change. Just as a patient cannot be treated without admitting their illness, you cannot change your financial situation without admitting that you need to. Any harmful behavior or poor financial habit can be seen as a form of "mental illness." And this illness can only be treated through confrontation, acknowledgment, and the willingness to upgrade your internal system.

The Mind: Your Core Operating System

Your mind is the engine that drives your life. If you operate with outdated thoughts, your results will remain stuck in the past. It is your thoughts that shape your decisions, and your decisions define your reality. So, if you want a better life, you must begin by upgrading your way of thinking.

Think of it like installing a new operating system on your device—it allows you to work more efficiently, avoid errors, and achieve your goals seamlessly.

The Greatest Challenge

Let's be honest: changing your way of thinking isn't easy. It's like waging a battle against your old self, your long-standing habits, and the thoughts that have lived with you for years. But it is a battle worth fighting. Because if you don't, you miss the chance to transform. If you do, however, you open the door to something greater: a life that aligns with your dreams.

Where to Begin?

1. **Acknowledge Your Current Reality**: Be honest with yourself. Write down everything that bothers you financially and analyze the root causes of those problems.

2. **Question Your Thoughts**: What beliefs brought you here? How can you replace them with new, empowering ones?

3. **Commit to Growth**: Just as you prioritize updating your devices, make upgrading your mindset a priority. Read, learn, and consistently challenge yourself.

The Golden Rule

To achieve new results, you must think in new ways. Just as modern devices deliver better performance through advanced features, upgrading your thinking will open doors you never imagined existed.

Summary

Acknowledgment is the first key to real transformation. Facing yourself with honesty and admitting that your current reality is a direct reflection of your past thoughts and decisions is the boldest step you can take. This is not weakness—it's courageous awareness that you are the main player in your story, and only you can rewrite its chapters.

Picture your thoughts as clouds that rain down your reality; every drop was a decision you made at some point. If you want to change what blossoms in your life, you must first change the clouds themselves. Transformation doesn't come from waiting for better circumstances—it comes from resetting your mind to become a tool that serves you, rather than a prison that holds you back.

What you are today is not a coincidence; it is the result of a series of small and large decisions. To break this chain, you must be brave enough to challenge your usual patterns. Change is not a luxury—it is a necessity for those who aspire to achieve more.

So, stop searching for excuses or justifications, and start upgrading your internal operating system, just as you would with your devices. Because, quite simply, you cannot change your reality without first changing yourself. Choose to begin now, because tomorrow waits for no one.

X2: The Leaks

Seal Your Leaks First

Imagine wanting to fill a warm bathtub to unwind after a long day, but there's one simple problem: the drain is open. No matter how much water you pour in, the tub will never fill. Now, think of money the same way. You cannot save or multiply it if there are invisible leaks draining it away without your awareness.

Now picture something even more absurd: trying to inflate a balloon with a hole in it. Despite your repeated efforts, the air escapes. In the end, you'll get tired, frustrated, and eventually give up. Do you see the similarity? Sometimes, we drain our finances through unseen leaks, all the while struggling to earn more. But the simplest solution is to seal the leaks first.

Face the Truth

Financial leaks are not just numbers in your bank account. They are habits, daily decisions, and sometimes short-lived indulgences that sabotage long-term goals. Every time you pay for an unnecessary subscription, buy an overpriced coffee, or purchase something trivial that adds no real value to your life, you're keeping the drain open.

Ask yourself: Why do I spend on these things? Do they bring me lasting happiness, or are they fleeting moments of satisfaction?
Always remember: What drains your income isn't just the amount you spend but the randomness and lack of awareness behind your spending habits.

The Rule

Before asking how to grow your wealth, ask yourself: *"Where is my money going?"*

Steps to Start Closing the Leaks:

1. Identify the Leaks:

- Sit down and analyze your expenses. Divide them into "necessary" and "unnecessary."

- Necessary expenses are those you can't live without, while the rest are financial leaks.

- Ask yourself:

    - Do I really need all these entertainment subscriptions?

    - How often do I spend on coffee or eating out?

    - How much do I spend on clothes, gadgets, or electronics that add no tangible value to my life?

2. Seal the Leaks:

- Once you've identified unnecessary expenses, start eliminating them. It may seem simple, but it requires discipline and awareness.

- Don't fool yourself: You might think, "What's 50 here or 100 there?" But these small amounts add up to hundreds or even thousands over the months.

3. Reduce Your Expenses to 50% of Your Income:

- Don't ask me—or anyone else—how to do this, because only you have the answer.

- Deep down, everyone knows what they can cut back on: maybe it's the daily takeout meals, that costly coffee habit, or buying things just because they're "on sale."

- When you reduce your spending, you'll realize you have far more control than you thought. You're not stuck in an endless consumption loop—you always have the power to change.

Start Now: Redirect Your Life's Flow

Every time you close a financial leak, you'll feel as if you've regained control of your life's direction. The wasted flow of money will stop, hold steady, and then slowly rise, steadily but surely. It's not about how much money you have right now; it's about your ability to manage it, to prevent waste, and to redirect it toward what truly matters.

Don't see this step as deprivation but as an opportunity. Every dollar you save from waste becomes a partner in building your future. Every leak you seal is another step toward achieving financial balance, another step toward filling the tub.

Picture yourself a year from now, reflecting on what you've accomplished. You'll see the tub full, a reflection of your courage, the courage that drove you to start today and to make the decision that changed your course.

Because money, like water, doesn't wait. Either you take control of it, or it slips through your fingers. Sealing the leaks isn't just a simple act—it's a declaration: You deserve control. You deserve abundance.

Start now. Close the leaks. Watch the tub fill—slowly, but with confidence.

Summary

To take control of your finances, you must first address the points of waste in your spending. Conduct a thorough review of your spending habits, replacing randomness with conscious planning. Every step you take to seal financial leaks means regaining control over your money and turning it into a tool for achieving your future goals with stability and effectiveness. Start today by closing the leaks that hinder your progress.

X3: Flow

Make Your Life a River That Flows Without Ceasing

Have you ever wondered why the Amazon River is considered a symbol of greatness and sustainability? The answer lies not just in its immense size but in its greatest secret: continuous flow. The Amazon is not a river that originates from a single source; instead, it is fed by a vast network of over 1,100 tributaries, including 17 major ones of significant importance. These tributaries, no matter how small some may be, are the lifeblood that gives the Amazon its strength and beauty.

In our financial lives, we need to adopt this model. We need diverse flows that build, expand, and nourish our lives, just as tributaries sustain the Amazon.

The Secret of Diverse Flow

Take Amazon, the global giant, as an example. Its remarkable success doesn't come from relying solely on e-commerce but from its intelligent strategy of diversifying income streams:

- **AWS:** Cloud services that are reshaping technology.

- **Prime:** Subscriptions that turn customers into lifelong partners.

- **Digital Advertising:** A platform that converts visits into massive revenue.

- **Digital Streaming:** Services like Prime Video that enter every home.

- **Traditional Retail:** Stores like Whole Foods, because true diversification knows no boundaries.

   Amazon isn't just a company; it's a river of financial flows, each tributary feeding the other, creating an unstoppable current.

Your Life as a River: Building Personal Flow

To achieve greatness in your financial life, you cannot rely on a single source of income. A single source is like a river dependent on one spring; if it dries up, everything comes to a halt. Instead, build a network of tributaries. Make money flow to you from every direction, no matter how small these flows may seem at first.

The First Tributary Leads to the Second

The fascinating thing about income streams is that each new source acts like a small tributary joining your life's river. And once the flow begins, it opens the door to new tributaries:

- A small project might lead to a larger investment.

- A side skill could open opportunities for freelancing or teaching.

- A social network might introduce you to opportunities you didn't even know existed.

It's like an interconnected ecosystem: one tributary brings another, and one feeds the next.

Why Your Life Should Have Multiple Flows

1. Protection Against Crises:

- When one source stops, others keep flowing.

2. Psychological Strength:

- Diversified income streams provide a sense of security and confidence because you're not reliant on just one source.

3. Continuous Growth:

- Small tributaries eventually turn into large currents that fuel your goals and open new doors.

4. Financial Independence:

- Diversification is the shortest path to financial freedom, making you less dependent on a job or single source of income.

How to Start?

1. **Look for Nearby Opportunities:**
   - Often, the tributaries are right in front of you, but you fail to notice them. It could be a skill you have, a small project, or even a neglected idea waiting to be revived.

2. **Be Innovative:**
   - Look for unconventional and creative ways to generate income. Flow begins when you think outside the box.

3. **Invest in Yourself:**
   - Learn new skills, uncover hidden talents, and continuously improve yourself. Every investment in yourself becomes a new tributary to your life's river.

4. **Start Small, But Start:**
   - Don't wait for the perfect moment. Small tributaries are what build mighty rivers.

Financial Flow: A Philosophy for Life

Flow isn't just a financial strategy; it's a philosophy for living. View money as a continuous stream, not as something stagnant. Like the Amazon, which grows stronger through the diversity of its tributaries, you must fill your life with small flows that unite to create an unstoppable current.

Make every decision you take, every skill you develop, and every opportunity you discover a new tributary feeding into your life's river. One day, you'll look back and see that you've built a river that flows endlessly. Start now, because the current of success begins with a single step.

X4: Leadership

Managing Money Is More Important Than Money Itself

What is your dream car? The car you envision yourself driving, heading toward a destination you've always longed to reach. Now, imagine you have it. The car is right in front of you, shiny and ready to go. But there's a problem: you don't know how to drive.

Do you see the irony? Your dream car becomes worthless, a mere piece of metal and glass. It may even become a burden, as owning it without knowing how to operate it adds to your frustrations.

Now, imagine yourself in a desolate place—a barren desert or a frozen tundra. You find a helicopter, fueled and ready with the keys inside. It seems like the perfect rescue opportunity, doesn't it? But you don't know how to pilot a helicopter. Suddenly, this tool, meant to save you, becomes a real danger. Randomly trying to operate it could lead to a disaster far worse than staying stranded.

Money, like a weapon, can be a beneficial tool or a source of danger. Owning it may seem like the solution to all your problems, but it can become a curse if you don't know how to manage it. Many believe earning money is the ultimate goal, but in reality, it's just the beginning. Money managed recklessly can vanish faster than it arrived, leaving you in a worse situation than before.

Having money without knowing how to manage it is like owning a luxurious car without knowing how to drive or finding a helicopter in the middle of a vast desert without knowing how to take off. The potential might seem limitless, but without skill, the results could be catastrophic.

Money Management: An Essential Skill

Managing money isn't a luxury; it's an essential skill that separates success from failure, wealth-building from loss. Just as learning to drive requires training and practice, mastering money management demands an investment of your time and effort.

Why Managing Money Is More Important Than Earning It

Because money that isn't managed wisely doesn't last. You might excel at earning money, but without a clear plan, it will all slip away. Conversely, someone who manages a small amount wisely can grow it into a fortune.

Where to Start

Money management isn't instinctive—it's a science you can learn. These steps will guide you:

1. **Learn the Basics**

    - Create a budget: Define your priorities, distinguishing between necessities and areas where you can cut back. Keep your spending under control.

    - Track your expenses: Use financial apps or a simple notebook to document everything you spend. This exercise will make you more aware of your financial habits.

    - Understand the basics of investing: Learn the difference between assets that increase in value and liabilities that drain your finances. Start by gaining a basic understanding of investment markets.

2. **Monitor Your Spending Closely**

   Every penny you spend should have a purpose. Before making a purchase, ask yourself:

   - Is this necessary?
   - Will it add real value to my life?
     Answering these questions will help reduce unnecessary spending and redirect your money toward meaningful goals.

3. **Control Your Emotions**

   - Don't let excitement or impulse dictate your financial decisions.
   - Avoid emotional shopping or spending under pressure.
   - Take time to think before making any major purchase.

4. **Invest in Yourself**

   - Education is the investment that never fails: Read books about money management.
   - Enroll in courses and learn from expert advice.
   - Listen to others' experiences through podcasts or educational videos.

5. **Save Before You Spend**

   - Allocate 10-20% of your income for savings or investments before addressing any other expenses.
   - Start an emergency fund that covers 3-6 months of expenses to prepare for unexpected situations.

6. **Learn the Art of Negotiation**

    o   Negotiation isn't just for merchants; whether you're buying a product or dealing with a service provider, negotiation can save you significant amounts over time.

7. **Plan for Long-Term Goals**

    o   Set both short- and long-term financial goals.

    o   Start planning for retirement, even at the beginning of your career.

8. **Commit to Regular Review and Improvement**

    o   Revisit your financial plan regularly, and adapt it to changing circumstances.

    o   Monitor your progress and ensure you're steadily moving toward your goals.

Be the Leader of Your Money, Not Its Follower

Throughout history, no powerful army achieved victory without a wise leader at the helm. The leader is the army's spirit, mastermind, and the one credited with its triumphs due to their intelligence, bravery, and meticulous planning. Your relationship with money is no different: be the leader, and make your money your army. Every dollar is a soldier in your ranks, and you decide whether to waste it or deploy it strategically to strengthen your position and win life's battles.

Summary

Managing money isn't just about saving; it's an ongoing skill that requires learning and practice. By starting with these steps, you'll notice a gradual transformation in your relationship with money and gain confidence in your ability to shape your financial future.

Money is a tool, and management is the key. Money alone isn't the solution; it's how you manage it that makes the difference. Having money without a plan or the skill to manage it is like owning a plane without knowing how to fly it. It might give you a moment of pride, but it won't take you anywhere.

Start today with the most important question: How can I become the leader of my finances?

Because money managed wisely not only ensures its sustainability but becomes the means to change your life, fulfill your dreams, and build your future with confidence.

X5: Pretending

Don't Try to Live Like the Rich Before You're Wealthy

Imagine a harsh winter night, cold seeping into your bones, and you have a bed with a blanket that's too small to cover you. You can't stretch your legs freely, can you? Instead, you're forced to curl up, adjusting your body to fit the blanket, just to find the warmth you desperately need. This scene mirrors an old proverb: "Stretch your legs according to the length of your blanket."

But in reality, many ignore this wisdom. They try to stretch their legs beyond the blanket—not to find warmth but to pretend they have a larger blanket than they actually do.

Appearances Don't Create Wealth

From the outside, your life might look like that of the rich: stylish clothes, a sleek phone, a shiny car, and a home that exudes luxury. You might appear to be living in comfort and abundance. But behind this facade lies another story: mounting installments, accumulating loans, or a maxed-out credit card that gets fully drained each month. By the end of the day, your bank account barely covers the essentials.

The harsh truth? You're not living like the wealthy; you're merely trying to look the part. And worse, even the wealthy themselves don't live this way.

The Difference Between You and the Wealthy

True wealth comes with understanding money. The wealthy don't spend frivolously to impress others; they invest their money to generate more. You might spend all you have—and even more—just to appear as if you belong to their league, while the wealthy spend far less than they own, often less than 1% of their fortune on luxuries.

On the other hand, you might be spending 100%, or even 110%, of your income just to buy into an illusion. The result? Financial stress, never-ending debts, and an inability to move forward.

True Wealth Starts Within

Being wealthy isn't about buying expensive clothes or driving a fancy car. True wealth is having financial freedom—the ability to sleep at night without worrying about bills or installments. The wealthy don't build their fortunes through spending but through investing, planning, and prioritizing.

Every krone you spend on the appearance of wealth is a krone that distances you from actually becoming wealthy. Every poor financial decision today is a step backward for your future.

How to Avoid the Trap

1. **Redefine Luxury:**

    o   Luxury isn't looking wealthy; it's being financially secure.

    o   Set priorities: financial freedom matters more than fleeting extravagances.

2. **Focus on Building Assets, Not Appearances:**

    o   Instead of buying a new phone every year, consider a small investment that increases your income.

    o   Avoid purchasing a large house that drains all your income; invest in assets that grow your wealth.

3. **Match Your Appearance to Your Reality:**

    o   It's okay to look ordinary now, as long as you're working to become extraordinary in your financial future.

The Paradox You Must Understand

Trying to live like the wealthy before you're actually rich is a major contradiction. Even the rich don't live as people imagine: endless spending or constant flaunting. True wealth comes with wisdom—spending smartly, knowing when to invest, and when to hold back.

If you aspire to be wealthy, start by building the foundation of your wealth: save, invest, and minimize unnecessary displays. If you live just to look rich, you'll remain stuck in the cycle of spending that keeps you from achieving your goals.

Summary

Don't let appearances deceive you, and don't confuse being rich with looking rich. True wealth is having freedom, financial peace, and the ability to make decisions without constraints.

If you truly want to reach that level, stop chasing appearances and start chasing the reality that leads to genuine prosperity.

X6: Temporal Preference

How to Build Your Future While Resisting the Urge of the Moment

While reading the previous five lessons, did you feel the path was long or that it required more effort than you anticipated? Maybe boredom crept in, or you thought you could postpone taking action to another day. This is completely natural because, as humans, we are hardwired to be drawn to the present, to chase instant rewards that provide a quick burst of happiness, even if that happiness is fleeting.

This tendency is known as "temporal preference"—the strong desire to gain rewards now rather than wait for something greater and more meaningful later. As the renowned economist John Maynard Keynes wrote in *The General Theory*: *"The tendency to prefer the present over the future is at the heart of most economic problems."*

Temporal Preference: Happiness Now or Success Later?

Think about it: we always have two options.

- To spend money now on an expensive meal or an unnecessary gadget, simply for that fleeting sense of gratification.

- Or to delay that expense, invest the money, and let it grow, granting us financial freedom in the future.

At its core, temporal preference is a battle between two desires:

1. The desire for instant gratification.

2. The ambition to achieve a long-term goal.

Unfortunately, most people succumb to the first. We are captivated by what's right in front of us. As George Loewenstein pointed out:
"Humans aren't good at thinking long-term. This behavioral flaw makes them disregard the future, even though today's decisions shape tomorrow."

Temporal Preference: A Mirror of Our Daily Habits

Take a moment to reflect on your financial habits:

- **Excessive spending:** Do you buy things simply because they're available now?

- **Lack of saving:** Do you always convince yourself that you don't have enough money to save?

- **Fear of investing:** Do you say, "Risk isn't for me," but spend recklessly on fleeting pleasures?

All of these habits are manifestations of temporal preference. They are small, cumulative decisions, like drops of water filling a leaky bucket, until you eventually realize there's nothing left to build your future with.

The Successful Few

Why do millionaires and entrepreneurs succeed while others remain stuck? Because they master the skill of "delayed gratification."

Delaying gratification doesn't mean depriving yourself of happiness—it means investing today to live a better life tomorrow. Buying a stock or starting a small business, instead of purchasing the latest tech gadget, might not offer immediate joy but could bring long-term satisfaction.

A Simple Example: The Smart Money Journey

Imagine you have $1,000. You have two choices:

1. Buy an expensive gaming console now that will bring you happiness for a few months.

2. Invest the money in a startup's shares. It might take a year or two, but it could eventually grow to $5,000.

The decision is simple, yet it reflects how temporal preference influences your choices.

How to Overcome Temporal Preference

1. **Set Long-Term Goals:**

   - Without a clear vision of your future, you'll keep chasing instant rewards. Define what you want to achieve in one year, five years, or ten years.

2. **Bring the Future into the Present:**

   - Visualize yourself ten years from now. What kind of life do you want to live? Every decision you make today, no matter how small, either moves you closer to that goal or further away from it.

3. **Turn Money into a Game:**

   - Think of every dollar as a tiny soldier. Will you send it to a reckless battle where it's lost, or will you train and deploy it strategically to build a powerful army that brings you victories?

4. **Reward Yourself Smartly:**

   - It's okay to enjoy the present, but set rules: allocate a small portion for immediate pleasures and the larger share for saving and investing.

5. **Learn from the Successful:**

   - Read about entrepreneurs and millionaires. They all have one thing in common: patience and discipline.

Summary: An Investment in Yourself and Your Future

Temporal preference isn't your enemy; it's a challenge. A challenge to retrain your mind to see the bigger picture. Patience and discipline are the keys to turning today's small rewards into tomorrow's monumental achievements.

Always remember:
"Your decisions today are the building blocks of your future."
So start delaying gratification and investing in yourself, because the greatest successes in life begin with patience.

X7: Multiplication

How to Make Money Come Alive

In the depths of the universe lies the secret of life: the principle of multiplication. Humanity, and all living beings, thrive through this simple concept—growth and reproduction. But have you ever considered that money, too, has the ability to multiply? Not through magic, but in a logical and straightforward way. Money isn't just numbers in your bank account; it's a seed. If you plant it in the right soil and nurture it with care, it can grow into a tree, laden with fruits that carry new seeds.

Money Loses Value if It Doesn't Renew Itself

Money that doesn't move diminishes. It may sound counterintuitive, but it's true. Inflation, obligations, and daily needs slowly erode its value. The only solution? Make money a living entity that multiplies. Not through miracles, but through investment, trade, or innovation.

Imagine every coin or bill you own has the potential to reproduce, but it's waiting for you to provide the right environment to start the process. The question is: Will you let your money remain dormant, or will you give it the chance to grow into an army that supports your ambitions?

The Story of Multiplication: How to Start from Scratch

Let me share a real story I experienced during the COVID-19 crisis. My professional life was collapsing before my eyes. The cleaning company I managed went bankrupt, and my online platform, which I considered an additional income source, was shut down. When the crisis ended, I faced a harsh reality: no income, no clear plan, and no desire to return to being an employee.

I decided to start a new cleaning company, but I needed at least $10,000—a sum I didn't have. I had two options: accept a situation I didn't choose or start anew with a simple idea, even if it seemed crazy or uncertain.

A bold idea struck me: Why not start a small business trading used items? I began by purchasing a used trailer from Finn, a well-known platform in Norway, for $1,000. I immediately listed it for resale at $2,000. Within ten days, I sold it for $1,800 after deducting $200 for advertising.

I repeated the process, and over time, the money began to "multiply" before my eyes. In just three months, I had accumulated the $10,000 I needed to launch my new company. The beginning wasn't perfect, but it was enough to change my life completely.

Your Personal Big Bang

Life, as we know it, began from nothing—a big bang. You, too, have the ability to create your own intellectual explosion, no matter how small it may seem at first. The simple idea that comes to your mind today could be the explosion that transforms your reality. All you need is to believe it's worth pursuing and to take the first step toward making it happen.

The Lesson: Profound Yet Simple

Just as business owners hire people to work for them, you can hire your money to work for you. Imagine every dollar you own is a tiny employee waiting for your instructions. Will you let it sit idle in a bank account, or will you set it to work and grow?

Money Is an Employee, Not a Master

Money isn't a tool that controls you; it's an employee that works for you. Your role as a leader is to create a plan to ensure this employee generates the highest possible return. As Robert Kiyosaki famously said in *Rich Dad Poor Dad*:
"Money should work for you, not the other way around."

How to Start Financial Multiplication

The methods are many, and the choice depends on your skills and goals:

- **Investing:** Stocks, real estate, or any asset that appreciates over time.

- **Trading:** Even a small-scale trade, like buying and selling used items, can serve as a solid foundation for your success.

- **Innovation:** One fresh idea could completely alter your life's trajectory.

- **Smart Saving:** Allocate a portion of your income for future investments.

Money as a Living Entity

Money isn't just numbers; it's energy. Like any energy, if you keep it trapped, it dissipates. But if you release it in the right direction, it grows and thrives.

Conclusion

True wealth begins with an idea—an idea that sees money not merely as a tool for spending but as a resource that can grow and work for you. Set your money in motion, provide it with the right environment, and let it multiply like life itself.

Just as life began from nothing with a great explosion, you, too, can start from scratch with a simple yet powerful intellectual burst. Choose to begin today, because money loves movement, and you are the leader who decides its direction.

X8: Selection

The Art of Choosing Your Future

In life, we are surrounded by countless options, but not all are equal in value or impact. Selection is not a random act—it's a conscious process, like pinpointing the right coordinates on a complex map. It's the ability to make smart, cohesive decisions aligned with your goals, rather than satisfying fleeting desires.

By nature, we are selective; we choose the clothes we wear, the food we eat, and the movies we watch. Yet, here lies the irony: most of us make choices based on what we want now, not on what we need to achieve our long-term goals.

Selection: Desire or Purpose?

Consider this simple example: when you visit a restaurant for the first time, you carefully browse the menu and pick something that satisfies your immediate craving. But what if you had a specific health goal? If you're aiming to lose weight, you'd choose a low-calorie dish. If you're building muscle, you'd opt for a protein-rich meal. In this case, your goal reshapes your decision-making process.

This simple model applies to every aspect of your life:

- **At work:** Are you choosing opportunities that support your career aspirations?

- **In relationships:** Are you surrounding yourself with people who uplift your goals?

- **In investments:** Are you selecting projects that provide long-term value?

Choosing the Right People: The Key to Success

One of the most sensitive aspects of selection is choosing your social and professional relationships. Your network and connections significantly shape your journey. You must be discerning about the people you allow into your life. Ask yourself: Are these individuals propelling me toward my goals, or are they hindering my progress?

The people you choose should be:

- Supportive of your ambitions.

- Capable of adding value to your life.

- Inspiring and helpful in your personal and professional development.

As the saying goes: *"If you're the smartest person in the room, you're in the wrong room."*

A strong network isn't just about friends who share enjoyable moments; it's about individuals you can rely on to help you achieve your goals.

Selection in Life: Beyond People

Selection doesn't stop at your social circle; it extends to everything that influences your path:

- **Your goals:** Are they clear and well-defined?

- **Opportunities:** Are you investing your time and energy in opportunities that align with your aspirations?

- **Behaviors:** Are your daily actions consistent with the values you believe in?

- **Knowledge:** Are you learning and reading in ways that align with your vision for the future?

Selection is a lens through which you can reorder your priorities. It's the art of determining what deserves your time, effort, and resources—and what you should ignore or let go of.

Is Success Possible Alone?

Ask a simple question: Has anyone in history achieved great success entirely on their own?

The answer is undoubtedly no. Every remarkable success story results from conscious selection of people, opportunities, and decisions.

- Successful entrepreneurs choose partners who share their vision.

- Major corporations rely on meticulously selected teams.

- Big goals are only realized through small, calculated decisions made consistently over time.

The Intelligence of Selection: How to Master It

1. **Align Your Choices with Your Goals:**

    o   If your choices don't support your goals, you're wasting time and energy.

2. **Be Selective with Your Network:**

    o   Surround yourself with individuals who inspire and guide you toward achieving your vision. Don't let randomness dictate your social life.

3. **Say "No" to What Doesn't Serve You:**

    o   Smart selection means having the ability to decline opportunities, relationships, or options that don't add value.

4. **Focus on Quality, Not Quantity:**

    o   Whether you're building a team, forming friendships, or choosing a reading list, prioritize the few that are meaningful over the many that are random.

5. **Regularly Reassess Your Choices:**

    o   Do your past decisions still align with your goals? Selection is not a one-time decision—it's an ongoing process.

Conclusion: Selection Makes the Difference

Selection isn't an ordinary skill; it's a strategic art that defines the quality of your life. Success doesn't come solely from luck or effort but from your ability to make intelligent, well-thought-out decisions at every stage.

Be mindful of every choice, because the future isn't built on randomness. Conscious selection is the gateway to sustainable success.

X9: The Center of the Circle

Just as the Earth revolves steadily around its axis, holding its core at its depth, and just as the sun orbits its path, adhering to the gravitational center that binds the universe together, our lives, too, must revolve around a clear and steadfast center. This center is the point of balance where your goals, thoughts, and behaviors converge to form a cohesive and harmonious system.

Just as the Earth or the sun drifting from their centers would result in chaos, the absence of a clear center in your life leads to randomness and deviation from your path. The center of the circle provides stability and clarity, guiding you toward what you desire without losing your way.

The Center of the Circle: The Starting Point for True Success

Imagine your life as a complete circle, with the essence of your goals and desires residing at its center. This center is not just a fleeting idea but the driving force that determines the direction of your entire life. Everything around you—decisions, actions, relationships—revolves around this center, and its quality is determined by how close or far it is to this pivotal point.

Thought: The Starting Point

Thought is the core of everything you are now and everything you hope to become in the future. Yet many fall into the trap of focusing on what they don't want, such as fear of debt, failure, or an uncertain future. These negative thoughts transform into emotions and actions that mirror this thinking, creating a vicious cycle of negative results.

The key lies in reprogramming the essence of your thinking to be positive and directed toward what you want to achieve. Focus solely on your goals, not your fears. If your thoughts start to veer off track, imagine a mental circle with your core goals at the center and a perimeter that keeps you from straying far from it. As long as your thoughts stay within this boundary, you're in a safe zone. If they wander beyond this range, pause immediately, reassess, and redirect your focus to the center.

Applying the Center of the Circle in Different Life Aspects

1. **Social Relationships: A Circle of Support and Harmony**
   Just as your thinking shapes your life's core, your relationships form the circle that surrounds you. Define the center of this social circle based on your personal values and goals.

   - Who aligns with this center?

   - Who drains your energy and pulls you away from your objectives?

   The relationships closest to your circle's center should be those that reinforce your values and propel you forward. Surface-level or negative relationships that fall outside this perimeter often hinder your progress. Evaluate them wisely and let go of what doesn't serve you without hesitation.

2. **Financial Goals: A Circle of Smart Investment and Spending**
   The money you have is not just numbers; it's a tool to achieve your goals. Assign a circle to each financial goal. Define a clear core for each circle, such as financial freedom or starting a successful project. Then, set a perimeter that represents the timeframe or budget you commit to.

   Every financial decision, whether investment or spending, should draw closer to this circle's center. If your financial choices stray outside this range, you risk wasting your resources without making real progress.

Creating Your Own Circles

You can apply the principle of the center of the circle to any aspect of your life:

- **Health:** Make the center of your health circle your primary goal, such as maintaining physical fitness or improving your lifestyle. Define the perimeter through habits that support this goal.

- **Professional Development:** Set the core of your career circle on achieving a specific objective, like advancing in your job or gaining new skills, and focus on activities that revolve around this center.

- **Time Management:** Prioritize your day within a time circle, placing the most important tasks closest to the center, and the less critical ones farther out.

Maintaining Balance in Your Circles

The center of the circle is not fixed; it's flexible and evolves as your goals and circumstances change. What remains constant is the necessity for all your actions and decisions to align with this center. If you feel you're drifting away from the circle's frame, pause immediately and recalibrate your course.

Conclusion

The "center of the circle" is more than just a concept; it's a way of life that helps you achieve clarity and balance in your decisions. When you create your own circles in various aspects of life and assign each one a center reflecting your values and goals, you'll find yourself more focused and capable of advancing toward success.

Always remember: the center is the beginning and the end. The clearer and more defined your core goals are, the easier it becomes for your life to revolve around them in harmony and balance.

X10: The Golden Standard

Development, Innovation, and Continuity

The nine previous principles lay a strong foundation for success, but there are three essential elements that make these principles more effective and sustainable: development, innovation, and continuity. These elements are not merely supplementary tools—they are the fuel that keeps you on track and ensures you achieve your aspirations in the best possible way.

First: Development – The Foundation of Survival and Growth

Development is an indispensable necessity in a rapidly changing world. Nature offers the greatest lessons in development: living organisms adapt their genetics to survive in their environments, and successful companies evolve to stay competitive.

Consider a real-world example: Nokia, once a dominant force in the mobile phone market, collapsed because it failed to adapt to rapid technological advancements. The lesson here is simple: if you stop developing, you set yourself on a path of decline.

You, too, need continuous development. Reading this book—or any book—won't be enough; you must make learning and self-improvement a daily habit. Strive to be better than you were yesterday, whether it's in your skills, ideas, or strategies.

Second: Innovation – The Difference That Makes Success

Innovation is the driving force behind every great idea. It turns the impossible into tangible, remarkable realities. Innovation doesn't necessarily mean creating something entirely new; it's about thinking unconventionally and using what you have in creative ways.

A Global Example:

Red Bull used a simple yet highly effective marketing innovation by scattering thousands of empty cans in busy public spaces. This made people believe everyone was drinking Red Bull, significantly boosting product demand.

A Personal Example:

When I launched my cleaning company, I faced intense competition from major companies with massive marketing budgets. Sales were weak in the first year, and I realized I needed an innovative strategy to capture attention.

That's when the idea of "Rengo," a Labrador retriever representing the company, was born:

- I created humorous images of Rengo dressed in cleaning gear and posted funny content on social media.

- I adopted a real Labrador and named him Rengo, sharing his "employment" story with the company as an official team member.

- I added Rengo's image to the company's vehicles, drawing attention on the streets and sparking widespread curiosity.

The results?

- A 1373.32% increase in sales in the second year.

- Massive social media engagement as people fell in love with Rengo's character and interacted with his posts.

- Local fame, turning the company into a popular topic in the community.

This innovation wasn't costly, but it relied on understanding the audience and leveraging resources in unconventional ways.

Third: Continuity – The Foundation for Achieving Ambitions

Even with development and innovation, success cannot be attained without continuity. Continuity means committing to working on your goals daily, regardless of obstacles or immediate results.

How to Achieve Continuity:

1. **Discipline:** Make working toward your goals a daily habit.

2. **Flexibility:** Don't stop when faced with challenges; instead, adapt your plans and adjust to circumstances.

3. **Belief in Your Ambition:** Always remember why you started and let your vision for the future drive you to persist.

The Golden Standard Summary

Development, innovation, and continuity are the three elements that transform the nine principles into a comprehensive system for success. They are the golden standard that ensures you achieve your goals in a sustainable and ever-evolving way.

"It's not enough to start—you must develop, innovate, and persist. With this approach, success becomes a matter of time, not luck."

Continuity: The Secret That Unites the Greatest Minds Towards Success

Psychologists on Continuity

Carl Jung:
"Success does not come from the ability to start but from the ability to persist despite all challenges."

Martin Seligman (Pioneer of Positive Psychology):
"Continuity is the key to developing positive habits that lead to a fulfilling and productive life."

William James:
"Continuous change, even if slow, creates a radical transformation over time."

Entrepreneurs on Continuity

Elon Musk:
"When you love what you do, you'll keep going even when things get tough. Continuity is what separates dreams from reality."

Steve Jobs:
"I am convinced that half of what separates successful entrepreneurs from unsuccessful ones is persistence."

Jeff Bezos:
"Great success requires a mix of innovation and continuity, but the most important factor is having patience during the process of building."

Leaders on Continuity

Winston Churchill:
"Success is not final, and failure is not fatal; what matters is the courage to continue."

Theodore Roosevelt:
"Do what you can, with what you have, where you are, and keep trying."

Nelson Mandela:
"Continuity was the drive that helped me resist imprisonment and injustice and believe that victory was possible."

Billionaires and Experts on Continuity

Warren Buffett:
"Perseverance builds wealth. Success in investment, as in life, is an ongoing process based on repeated and correct decisions."

Richard Branson:
"Nothing worthwhile can be achieved without continuity. Try, fail, and then try again."

Jack Ma (Founder of Alibaba):
"Today is hard, tomorrow will be harder, but the day after tomorrow will be bright. Success comes only if you persist."

Management and Development Experts on Continuity

Peter Drucker (Father of Modern Management):

"Continuity means committing to goals even if results are not immediate. It's the cornerstone of effective management."

John C. Maxwell (Leadership Expert):

"Continuity is not a burden; it is a testament to believing in what you do."

Stephen Covey (Author of *The 7 Habits of Highly Effective People*):

"Small daily habits, practiced consistently, lead to great successes over time."

Summary

Continuity is not just a passing trait; it is the common denominator of all success stories. As highlighted by these experts and leaders, perseverance and patience are the core factors in achieving ambitions and overcoming challenges.

"Continuity is the thread that weaves the fabric of success, transforming dreams into reality through unwavering effort and commitment."

10X1,000,000: Implementation

"*What you have read in this booklet is not merely words on paper—it is a philosophy that I began applying in my own life. As I learned from the principles outlined here, success is not only about achieving personal goals but also about multiplying your impact to benefit others and the world around us.*"

For this reason, I decided to make this very booklet a living example of what it advocates. I am now applying a smart marketing idea mentioned between its lines, turning your purchase of this booklet into a step toward multiplied benefit. **Half of the profits from this booklet will be directed toward two noble causes:**

1. **Planting One Million Trees:**
   Giving back to the Earth is a true investment in our shared future. The country where the trees will be planted will be chosen through your votes.

2. **Supporting Shelter for Stray Animals:**
   Contributing to humanitarian projects aimed at treating and sheltering stray animals in developing countries, because true humanity is reflected in protecting the most vulnerable among us.

But there is something even deeper. By reading these words and purchasing this booklet, you are not only gaining the tools to improve your life but also becoming a partner in this journey. More importantly, you contribute to spreading this booklet because, naturally, you will find yourself eager to share it with others—not just for its practical benefits but for the charitable and humanitarian message it carries.

In doing so, I am practicing the ideas from this booklet about smart marketing and positive impact. You, in turn, become part of this never-ending chain.

Let's Be Part of This Movement Together

- **Benefit from the ideas, contribute to the good, and spread the message.**

- *Because true success is the kind that multiplies to include everyone.*

"True success is not measured by what you achieve for yourself but by what you add to the world around you."
"Every great idea holds the power to create change, but it requires courage to be implemented."

Thank you for reading!
We value your feedback. Share your thoughts with us: **@DantonDark**

www.ingramcontent.com/pod-product-compliance
Lightning Source LLC
Chambersburg PA
CBHW062124220526
45471CB00010B/3874